J
745.
592
WAL

Wallace, Mary
I Can Make Games

$14.96

DATE DUE			

5/96

I Can Make

GAMES

written and photographed by

Mary Wallace

Owl Books

I Can Make Games

Owl Books are published by Greey de Pencier Books Inc.,
179 John Street, Suite 500, Toronto, Ontario M5T 3G5

Owl and the Owl colophon are trademarks of Owl Communications.
Greey de Pencier Books Inc. is a licensed user of trademarks of Owl Communications.

Distributed in the United States by Firefly Books (U.S.) Inc.,
230 Fifth Avenue, Suite 1607, New York, NY 10001.

This book was published with the generous support of the Canada Council,
the Ontario Arts Council and the Government of Ontario through
the Ontario Publishing Centre.

Canadian Cataloguing in Publication Data

Wallace, Mary, 1950–
I can make games

ISBN 1-895688-28-0 (bound) ISBN 1-895688-29-9 (pbk.)

1. Games - Juvenile literature. I. Title.

GV1203.W35 1995   j790.1'922   C94-932076-5

Design & Art Direction: Julia Naimska
Cover photo, center: Ray Boudreau

Games on the front cover, counterclockwise from upper left:
mice and cheese from Cat and Mouse; Feed the Shark; Mini Golf; Trip Kit.

The crafts in this book have been tested and are safe when conducted as instructed.
The author and publisher accept no responsibility for any damage caused or sustained
by the use or misuse of ideas or material featured in the crafts in *I Can Make Games*.

Other books by Mary Wallace
I Can Make Toys
I Can Make Puppets
I Can Make Gifts
How to Make Great Stuff to Wear
How to Make Great Stuff for Your Room

Printed in Hong Kong

A   B   C   D   E   F

CONTENTS

LET'S MAKE GAMES

You can make and play all the games in this book. It's easy. It's fun. These two pages show the things used to make the games in this book, but you can use other things if you like. You'll find most of what you need around the house — get permission to use what you find. To play some of the games you'll need a place without things that might break or younger children that could get hurt. Play safely and have fun!

- aluminum foil
- white glue
- yarn
- milk or juice carton
- funnel
- Bristol board
- balloons
- spoon
- flour or fine sand

- bowl
- plastic bag
- acrylic paint
- bendable straw
- paintbrush
- cardboard box
- paper bags
- egg carton
- soil

- small boxes
- sponge
- face cloth
- tape
- stapler
- cardboard
- light-weight chain
- beads
- star stickers
- foam tray
- plastic wrap
- markers

- construction paper
- tracing paper
- paper tubes
- masking tape
- hole punch
- rubber bands
- buttons
- bottle caps
- scissors
- paper clips

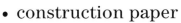

- envelopes
- soft lead pencil
- chalk
- pencil crayons
- die
- googly eyes
- toy shovel
- fabric marker
- candies
- shoe box
- felt

5

TANGLE

- 2 milk or juice cartons
- scissors
- masking tape
- six colors of construction paper
- pencil
- white glue

①

cut two square
boxes from
carton bottoms

cut

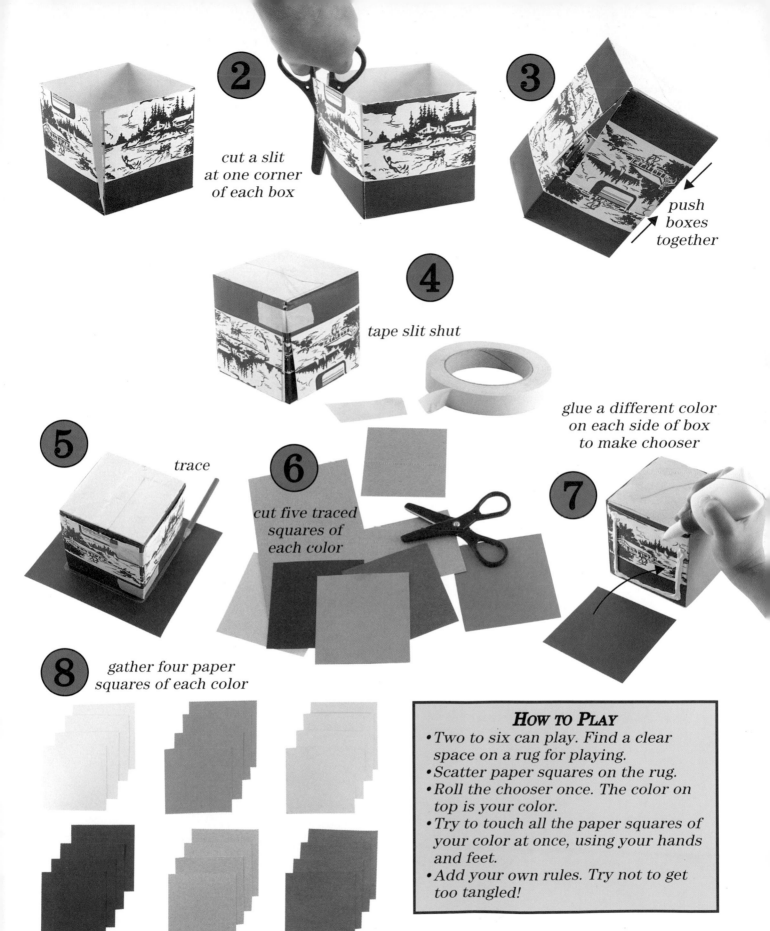

2 cut a slit at one corner of each box

3 push boxes together

4 tape slit shut

glue a different color on each side of box to make chooser

5 trace

6 cut five traced squares of each color

7

8 gather four paper squares of each color

HOW TO PLAY

- Two to six can play. Find a clear space on a rug for playing.
- Scatter paper squares on the rug.
- Roll the chooser once. The color on top is your color.
- Try to touch all the paper squares of your color at once, using your hands and feet.
- Add your own rules. Try not to get too tangled!

7

HATCHING EGG

- tracing paper
- 2 paper clips
- soft lead pencil
- scissors
- Bristol board
- envelope

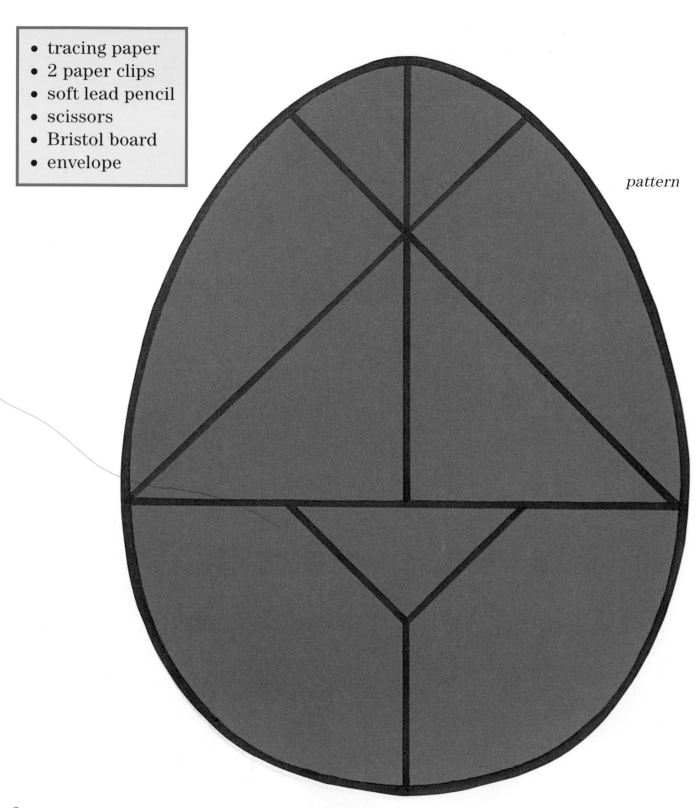

pattern

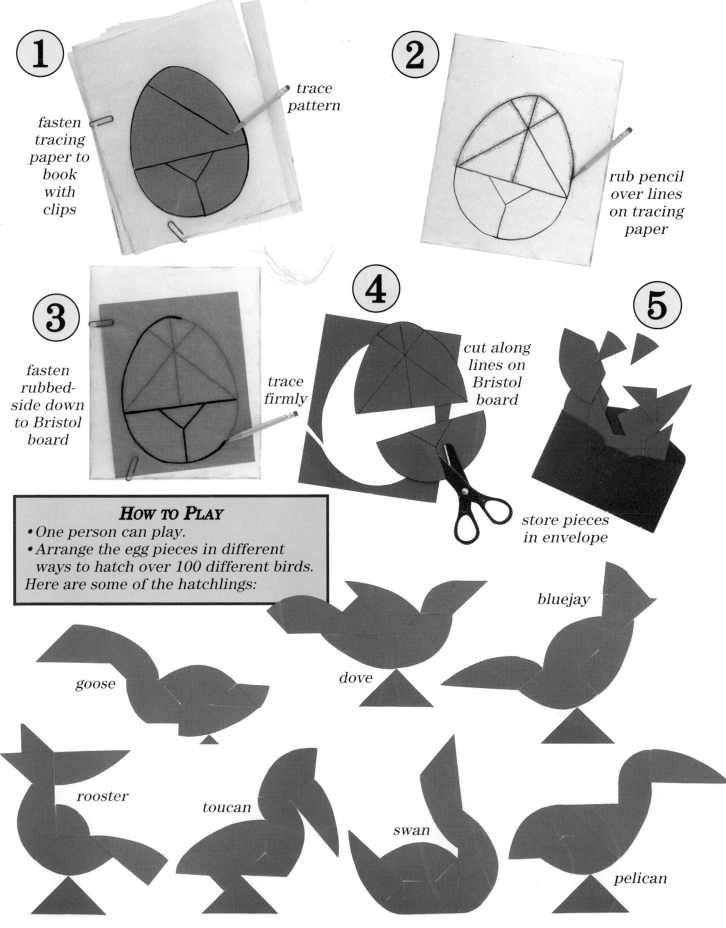

1 fasten tracing paper to book with clips

trace pattern

2 rub pencil over lines on tracing paper

3 fasten rubbed-side down to Bristol board

trace firmly

4 cut along lines on Bristol board

5 store pieces in envelope

HOW TO PLAY
- One person can play.
- Arrange the egg pieces in different ways to hatch over 100 different birds. Here are some of the hatchlings:

bluejay

dove

goose

rooster

toucan

swan

pelican

MONKEY RACE

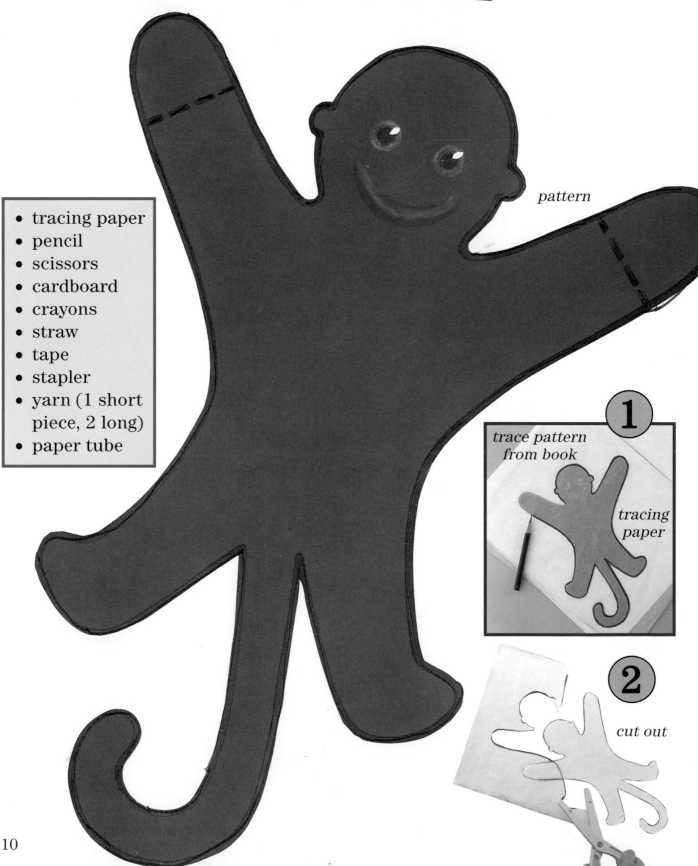

pattern

- tracing paper
- pencil
- scissors
- cardboard
- crayons
- straw
- tape
- stapler
- yarn (1 short piece, 2 long)
- paper tube

1 trace pattern from book

tracing paper

2 cut out

3
trace outline onto cardboard

4
cut out
decorate

5
cut two pieces of straw

6
fold over
tape straw pieces

7
staple
thread long pieces of yarn through straws
tie loops on ends

8
tie a short piece to middle
tie long pieces to end of tube

HOW TO PLAY
- Two or more play.
- Tie the short piece of yarn up high.
- Gently tug one loop, then the other, to make monkey climb.
- Make two and race!

SQUISHERS

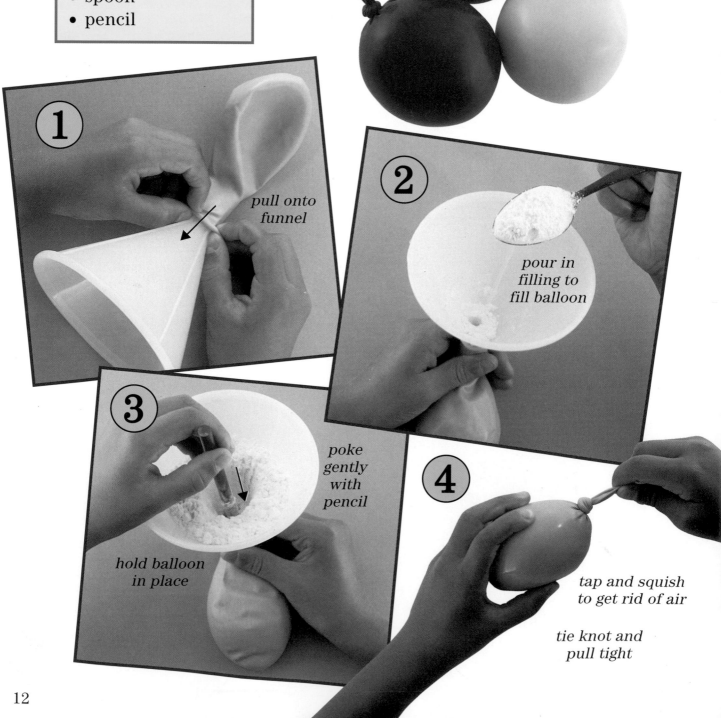

- large balloons
- fine sand or flour
- funnel
- spoon
- pencil

1 pull onto funnel

2 pour in filling to fill balloon

3 poke gently with pencil

hold balloon in place

4 tap and squish to get rid of air

tie knot and pull tight

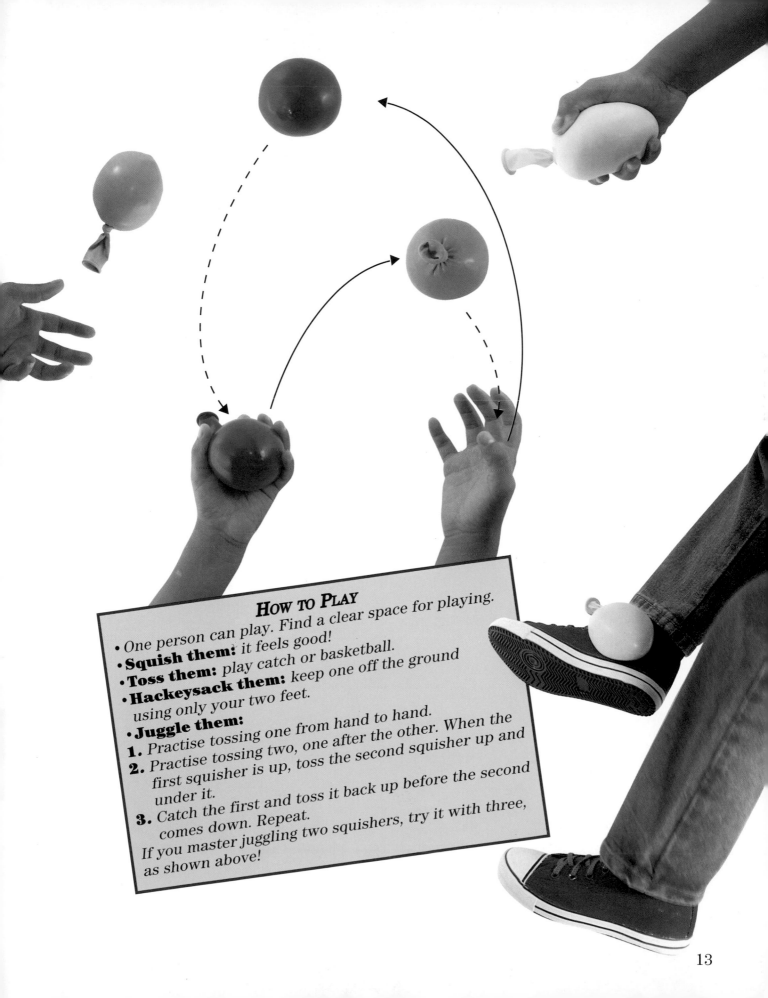

HOW TO PLAY

- One person can play. Find a clear space for playing.
- **Squish them:** it feels good!
- **Toss them:** play catch or basketball.
- **Hackeysack them:** keep one off the ground using only your two feet.
- **Juggle them:**
1. Practise tossing one from hand to hand.
2. Practise tossing two, one after the other. When the first squisher is up, toss the second squisher up and under it.
3. Catch the first and toss it back up before the second comes down. Repeat.

If you master juggling two squishers, try it with three, as shown above!

CAT AND MOUSE

- yellow sponge
- scissors
- egg carton
- acrylic paint
- paintbrush
- white glue
- yarn

- 8 googly eyes
- construction paper
- small box
- markers
- 1 large piece of Bristol board
- 1 die

CHEESE

cut sponge into ten triangle-shaped pieces

MICE

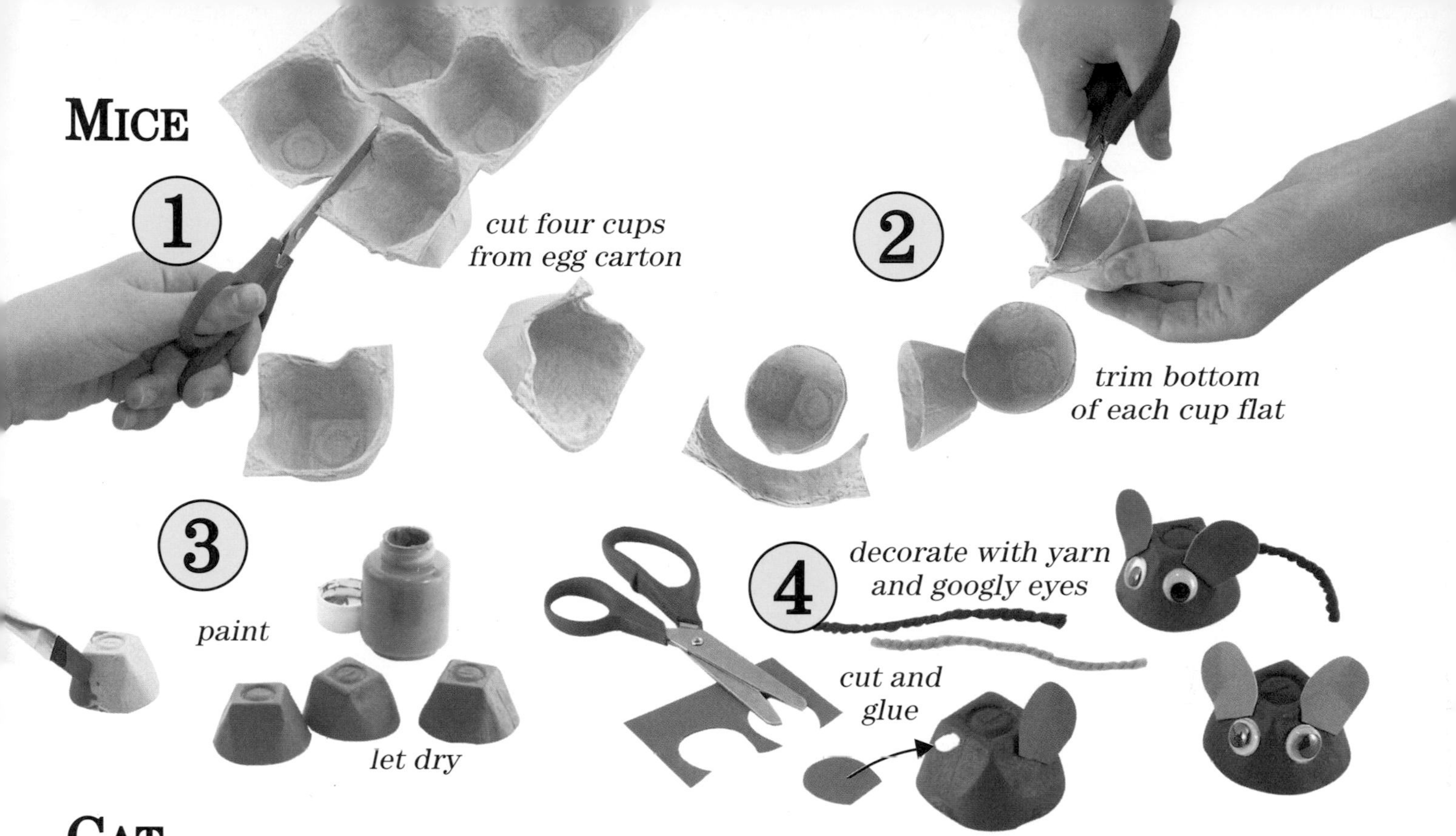

① cut four cups from egg carton

② trim bottom of each cup flat

③ paint

let dry

④ decorate with yarn and googly eyes

cut and glue

CAT

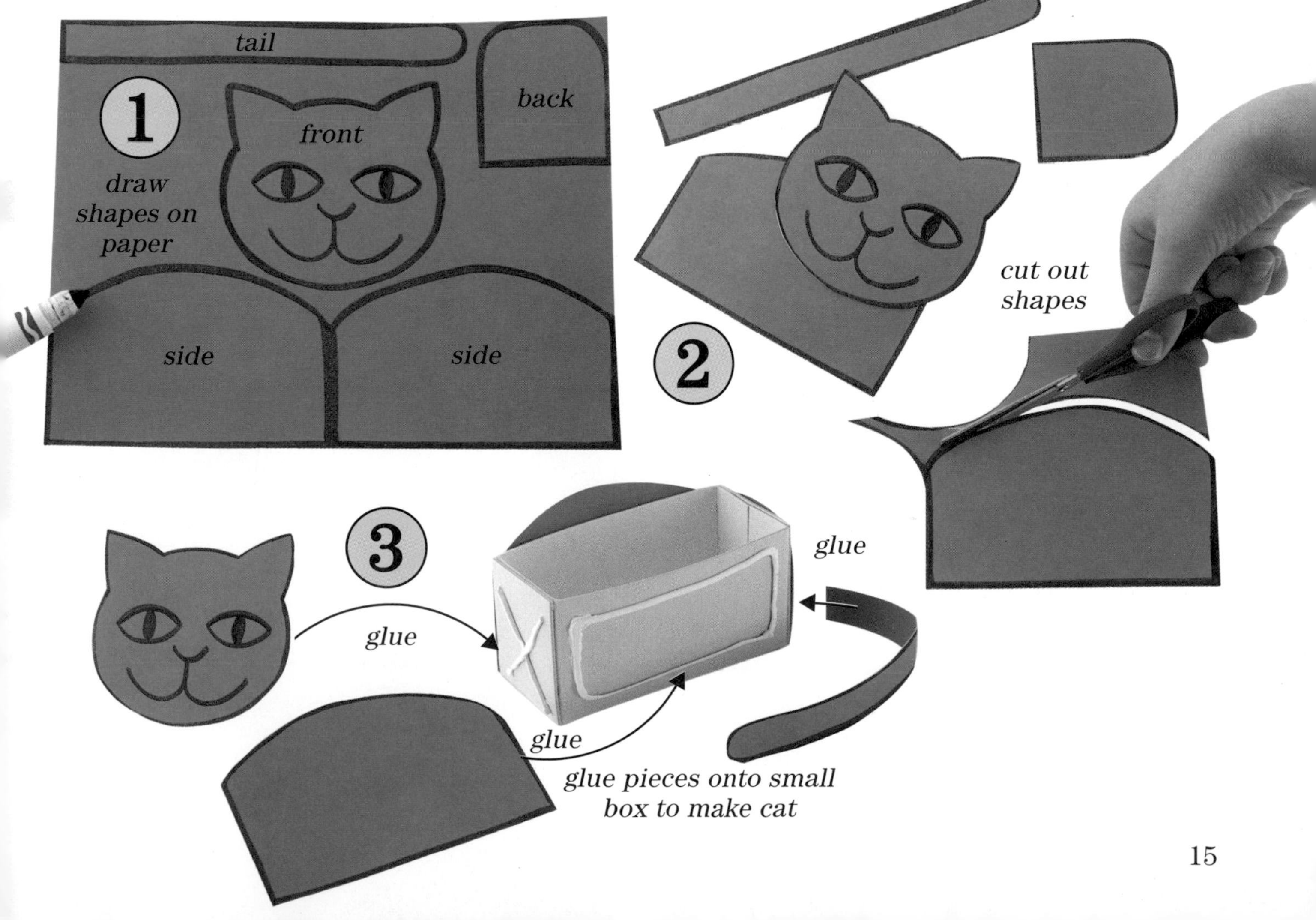

① draw shapes on paper

tail

back

front

side   side

② cut out shapes

③ glue

glue

glue

glue pieces onto small box to make cat

GAMEBOARD

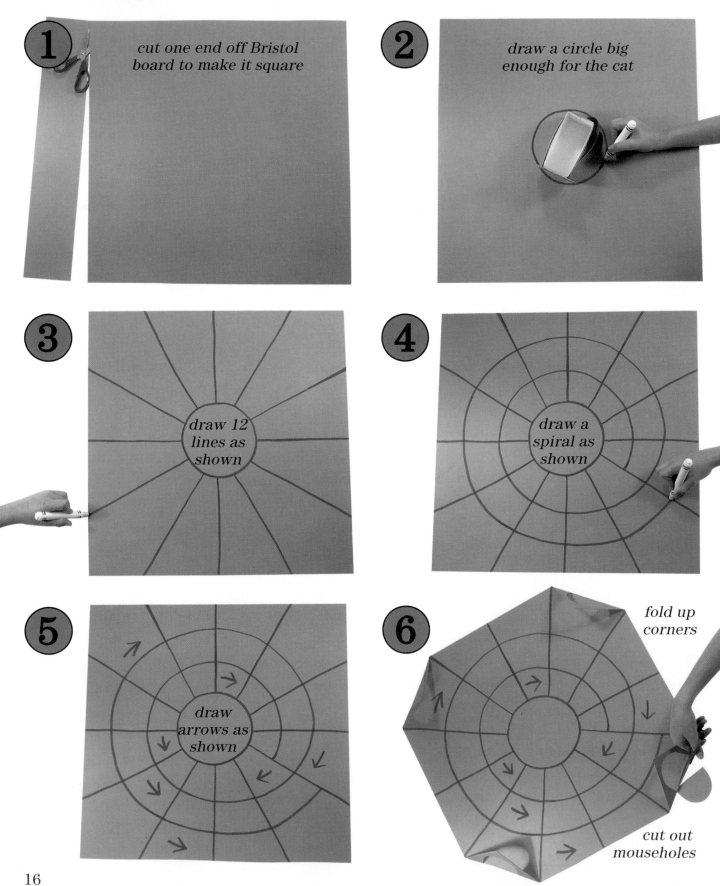

1 cut one end off Bristol board to make it square

2 draw a circle big enough for the cat

3 draw 12 lines as shown

4 draw a spiral as shown

5 draw arrows as shown

6 fold up corners

cut out mouseholes

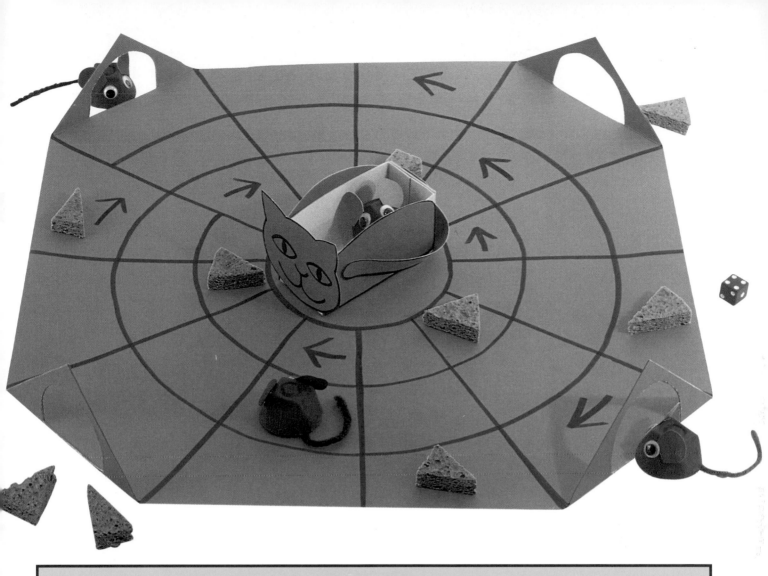

HOW TO PLAY

- Two or more play this cooperative game.
- Place the cat in the middle. Mice that land in the row of spaces directly in front of the cat are caught and go in the cat.
- Scatter cheese on the board. Mice start at the mouseholes.
- Take turns rolling the die. Choose any mouse and move along the spiral towards the center. If a mouse reaches the center, it turns around and returns to its hole.
- When your roll lands a mouse on the same square as a piece of cheese, the mouse picks up the cheese. The mice take

the cheese, one piece at a time, back to the mouseholes. After a mouse gets a piece of cheese into a hole, it starts again. All moves are by roll of die.

- When your roll lands a mouse on an arrow, the cat turns one space in the direction of the arrow. Any mice now in the row of spaces directly in front of the cat are caught and go in the cat.
- Players plan together to outsmart the cat! Try to get as many mice with their pieces of cheese as you can safely back into the mouseholes.

PIN BALL BOWL

- fat paper tube
- thin paper tube
- 5 short tubes
- acrylic paint
- paintbrush
- hole punch
- masking tape
- 2 rubber bands
- yarn
- aluminum foil

①

paint numbers on short tubes to make pins

fat paper tube

thin paper tube

②

punch holes as shown

fat paper tube

tape over end of thin tube

thin paper tube

3 attach rubber bands to fat tube

4 put thin tube inside

push rubber band ends through holes in thin tube

5 tie rubber bands together with yarn

6 crumple aluminum foil into balls

7

HOW TO PLAY

- Two or more play. Find a clear space for playing.
- Arrange pins in a "V" shape. Load ball, pull back the inside tube and let go to shoot ball. Add up the points printed on the pins you've knocked down.
- The player with the most points wins.

OWL EYES

- *adult to help punch holes*
- small box
- paper
- pencil
- scissors
- white glue
- foam tray
- hole punch
- 6 beads
- plastic wrap
- tape

1
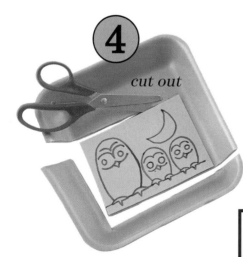
trace box onto paper

2

cut out

draw owls on paper

3

back

glue paper to tray

4

cut out

5
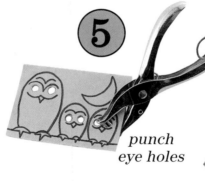
punch eye holes

6
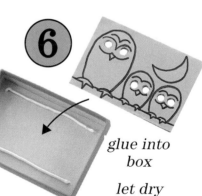
glue into box

let dry

8
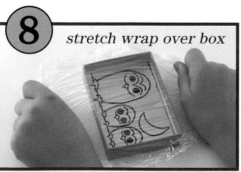
stretch wrap over box

9

tape around edges of wrap

7
put in beads

HOW TO PLAY
- One person can play.
- Shake box gently to roll beads into holes.

FEED THE SHARK

- Bristol board
- markers
- face cloth
- pencil
- light-weight chain
- tape

1 *draw shark and fish*

Bristol board

2 *poke two holes with pencil as shown*

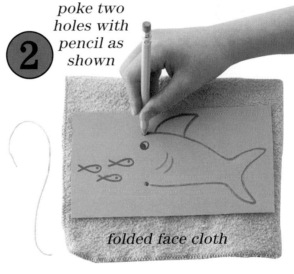

folded face cloth

3 *put chain ends through holes*

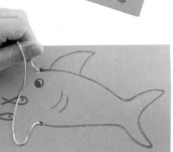

4

back

adjust chain length then tape ends

HOW TO PLAY
- *One person can play.*
- *Shake gently to open shark's mouth around fish.*

SIX MAN MORRIS

- colored paper
- scissors
- white glue
- cardboard
- marker
- 16 star stickers
- 6 buttons
- 6 bottle caps

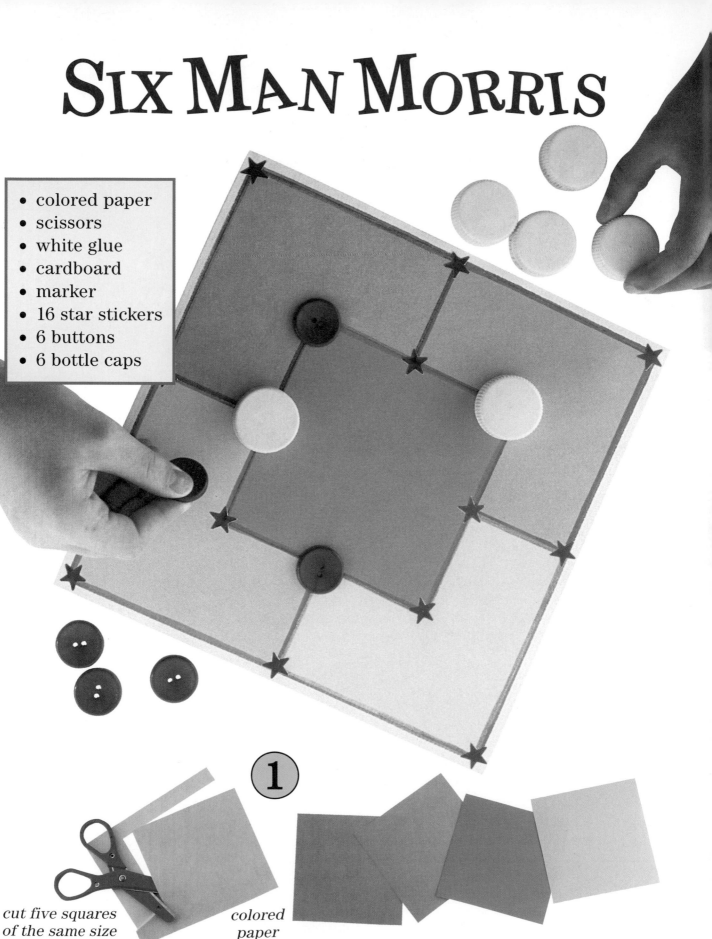

①

cut five squares of the same size

colored paper

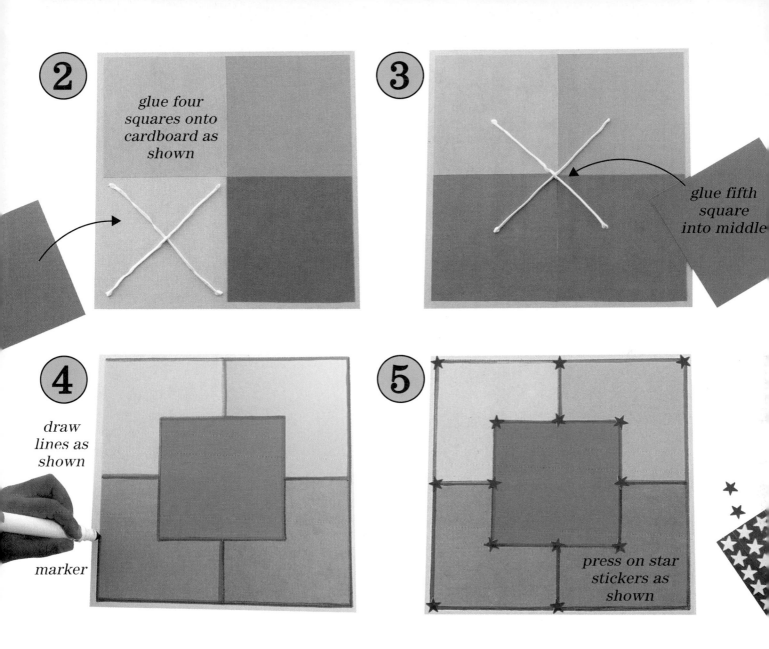

② glue four squares onto cardboard as shown

③ glue fifth square into middle

④ draw lines as shown

marker

⑤ press on star stickers as shown

HOW TO PLAY

- Two people play. The best way to learn this game is to play it!
- Each player has either six buttons or six bottle caps as playing pieces.
- Start by placing your pieces on uncovered stars. Take turns placing one piece on the board at a time.
- Throughout the game, try to get three pieces in a row along a line. These will be "safe." Any time you get a safe row of three on the board, you can take one of the other player's pieces, as long as it is not in a safe row.

- When a piece is taken, it is out of play. Once all your pieces are on the board or out of play, take turns moving your remaining pieces, one at a time. A piece can move along any line to an uncovered star next to it. (You can't make the same row of three more than once.)
- When you have only three pieces left, you can jump to any uncovered star on the board.
- You win when the other player has only two pieces left, or if you have blocked all the other player's moves.

23

MINI GOLF

HAZARDS

- 4 cardboard boxes
- pencil
- scissors
- Bristol board
- glue or tape
- acrylic paint and brush
- paper tube
- *decorate as you like*

ELEPHANT

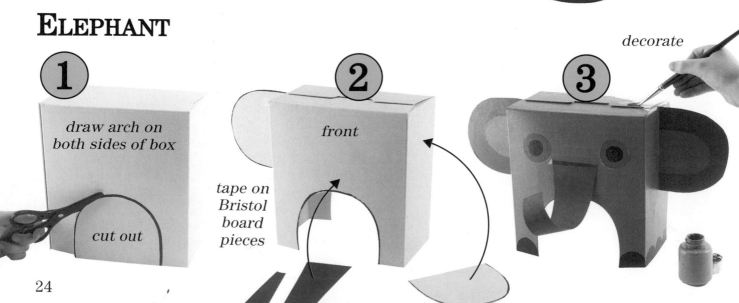

1 *draw arch on both sides of box*

cut out

2 *front*

tape on Bristol board pieces

3 *decorate*

HIPPO

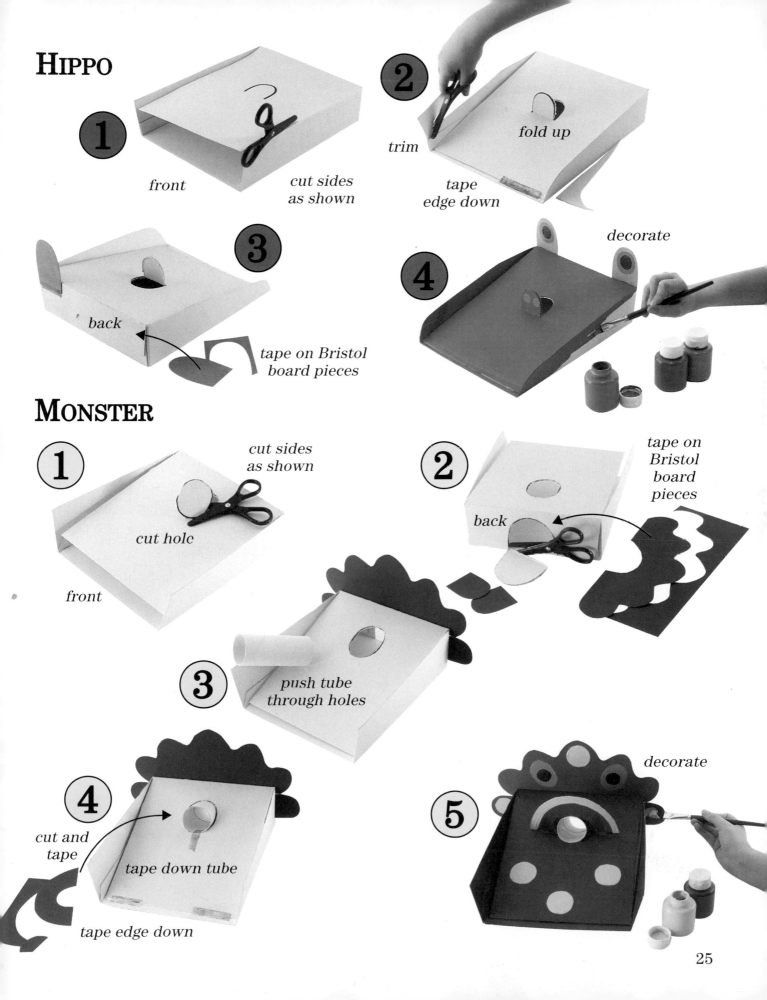

1 front / cut sides as shown

2 trim / tape edge down / fold up

3 back / tape on Bristol board pieces

4 decorate

MONSTER

1 front / cut sides as shown / cut hole

2 back / tape on Bristol board pieces

3 push tube through holes

4 cut and tape / tape down tube / tape edge down

5 decorate

CROCODILE

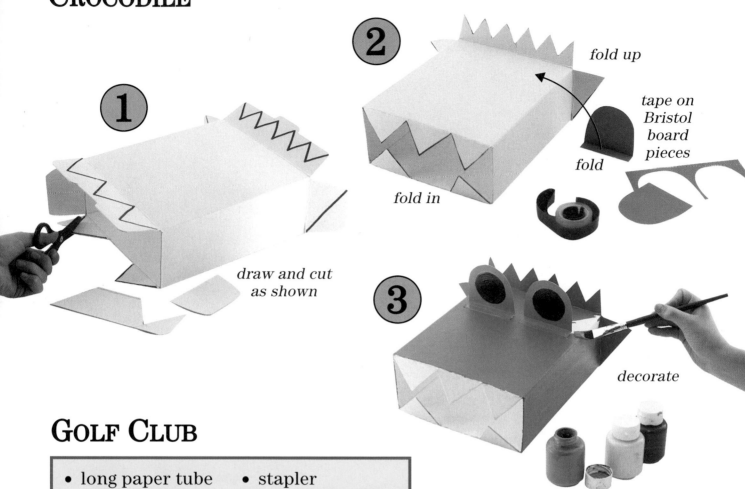

1 *draw and cut as shown*

2 *fold up* — *tape on Bristol board pieces* — *fold* — *fold in*

3 *decorate*

GOLF CLUB

• long paper tube	• stapler
• scissors	• acrylic paint
• short paper tube	• paintbrush

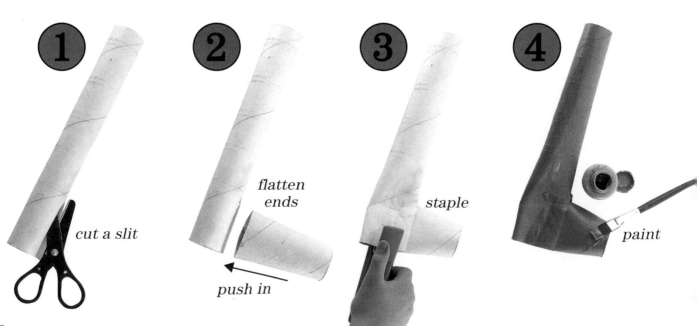

1 *cut a slit*

2 *flatten ends* — *push in*

3 *staple*

4 *paint*

CUP

- Bristol board
- scissors
- construction paper
- marker
- bendable straw
- tape

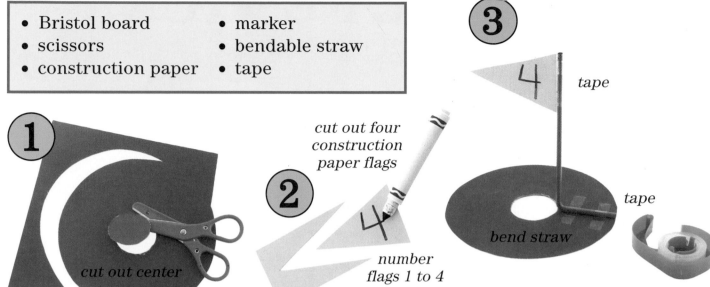

1 cut out center

cut circle from Bristol board

2 cut out four construction paper flags

number flags 1 to 4

3 tape

tape

bend straw

TEE

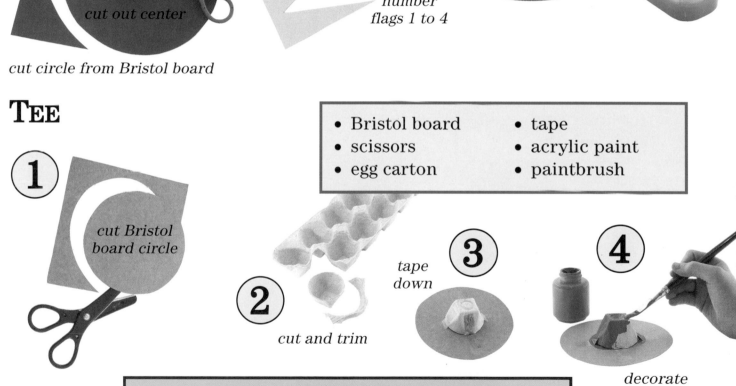

1 cut Bristol board circle

- Bristol board
- scissors
- egg carton
- tape
- acrylic paint
- paintbrush

2 cut and trim

tape down

3

4 decorate and dry

HOW TO PLAY

- Two or more play. Find a clear space for playing.
- Set up course: 1 tee, 1 hazard and 1 cup for each hole.
- Start by putting a small ball on the first tee. Hit the ball with golf club. Try to hit it through the hazard and then into the cup. Try to use as few hits as possible to get the ball into the cup.
- Your score is the number of hits it takes to get the ball in the cup.
- After everyone plays all four holes, total each player's scores. The lowest total score wins.

TREASURE HUNT

- *adult to give permission to dig*
- 2 brown paper bags
- soil
- water
- bowl
- plastic bag
- pencil crayons
- scissors
- envelope
- tape
- aluminum foil
- toy shovel
- treasure (candy, toys, books, etc.)

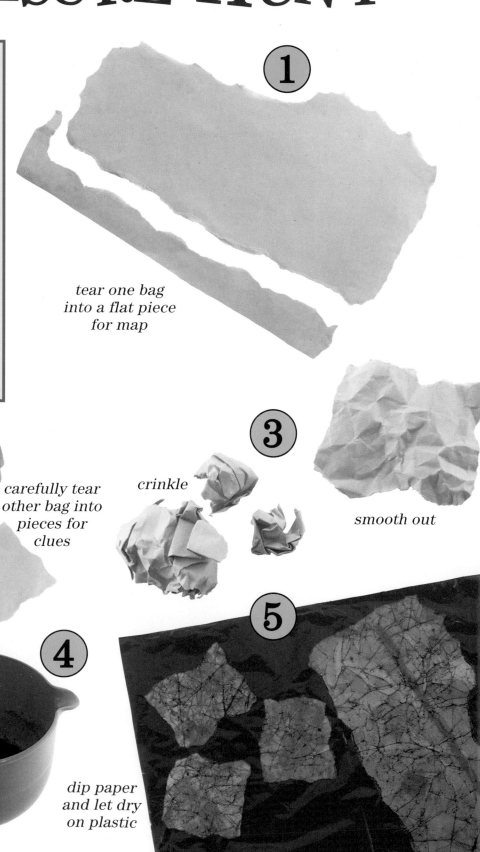

1 tear one bag into a flat piece for map

2 carefully tear other bag into pieces for clues

3 crinkle   smooth out

4 mix 2 spoons soil into a bowl of water

5 dip paper and let dry on plastic

6 decide where to hide clues and treasure

draw a treasure map

7 *write and number the clues*

① Climb the stairs to where you sleep. On the floor you'll have to creep.

② Find the tree that has a split. Stand on your toes and reach for it.

③ Come out here to rest your feet. Look underneath this cosy red seat.

8 *cut up the map*

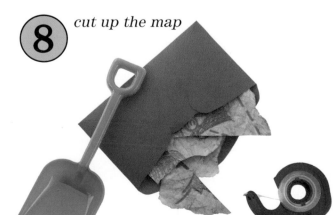

put pieces in envelope with a roll of tape

HOW TO PLAY

- Hide the treasure. If you want to bury it, wrap it in aluminum foil first. Get permission to dig.
- Hide map and clues #2 and #3. Clue #1 will lead to where clue #2 is. Clue #2 will lead to where clue #3 is. Clue #3 will lead to where the map is.
- Two or more play: treasure hider and one or more treasure hunters.
- Give clue #1 to the treasure hunters.
- The treasure hunters must find the clues in order, find the map, and then tape the map together. The map will lead the hunters to the treasure.

TRIP KIT

- *adult to help punch holes*
- shoe box with lid
- felt
- scissors
- white glue
- chalk
- fabric marker
- hole punch
- envelopes for storing pieces

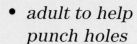

1

cut felt to fit box lid

2

glue felt to box lid

STORYBOARD

1

chalk

2

3 decorate

draw and cut shapes from felt

arrange pieces on box lid to make pictures and stories

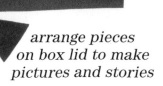

XS AND OS

cut a felt square

use marker to draw four lines as shown

①

cut four circles for Os

②

cut four squares and cut out corners for Xs

HOW TO PLAY
• *Two people play.*
• *Place square on box lid.*
• *One player takes Xs; the other player takes Os. Take turns putting your pieces on empty spaces.*
• *Three in a row going any direction wins.*

SOLITAIRE

cut felt square

draw lines as shown

①

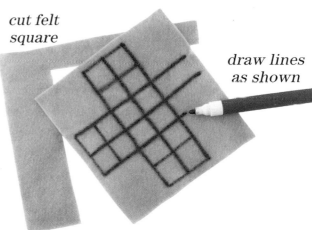

punch holes as shown

②

punch 32 circles of another color

HOW TO PLAY
• *One person can play.*
• *Place square on box lid.*
• *Put the felt circles into all the holes except the one in the center.*
• *At every move, jump one circle over one next to it, and remove the jumped circle. Keep jumping and removing circles until there are no jumps possible.*
• *End up with as few circles as you can.*